You Are My All

You Are My All

A Collection Of Personal Poems

Erhard Vogel

Nataraja Yoga Ashram
San Diego, California

Nataraja Yoga Ashram

Copyright © 2024 Erhard Vogel

Printed and bound in the United States of America. All rights reserved. No part of this book may be reproduced or transmitted in any form or by any means, graphic, electronic or mechanical, including photocopying, recording, taping or by an information storage and retrieval system, without the written permission of the author, except in the case of brief quotations embodied in critical articles or reviews. For information, please contact Nataraja Yoga Ashram, 10171 Hawley Road, San Diego CA 92021. First printing 2024.

ISBN 978-1-892484-14-7 (sc)
ISBN 978-1-892484-17-8 (e)
Library of Congress Control Number: 2024923176

Dedication

This book of personal poems is dedicated to all of you who have enriched my life. May you treat yourself with love and kindness to the fulfillment of your reason for Being.

–Erhard

Contents

The Quest
Now And Then 3
Important To Ponder And Know 5

Concerns
Woodstock 9
The Anguish Imposed By Fate 11
Her Anguish 13
As I Look Into Your Eyes 15
Behind My Wall 17
Karma 19
The Infinite Wayfarer 21
Soul's Dirge Of Despair 23

Deliverance
The Road To Liberation 27
Deliverance 29

Conscious Action
Choices 33
In The Joy Of Light 35
The Law Of Cause And Effect 37
Truth 39
We Are Interconnected 41
A Good Strategy 43

Empathy

Hear My Heart 47
Be Still My Heart 49
Empathy 51
Love Glows 53

Evolving

Evolve Or Perish 57
Simply Live Your Real Identity 59
The Power And Beauty Of Being 61
Human Life 63
Metamorphosis 65
Why Do You Tarry 67

Meditation

Endless Delight 71
Meditation 73
Nataraja 75
Focused In Serenity 77
Dwelling In The Unalloyed Experience Of Self ...79
The Eternal Now 81
Abiding Love 83

Interconnected Being

In The Garden 87
Busy Bee 103

Living The Light

All This I Am 107

Mirror Light 109
　　Absorbed In The Light Of Being 111

Love

　　A Perfect Romantic Moment 115
　　The Dance of Creation 117
　　Liberation 119
　　You Are My All 121
　　Concert 123
　　We Have Each Other 125
　　I Give Thanks 127

Sweet Death

　　A Wave 131
　　What Death Has Me Ask 135
　　Oh Death 137
　　Going Home 141
　　Free To Fly Past Stars And Galaxies 143
　　Now I Lie Here Sweet Death 145

I Am

　　I Am Infinite Being 149
　　I Am 151
　　I Am That 155
　　Experiencing Being Together 157

Photograph Captions 159
About The Author 161
Also By Erhard Vogel 165

The Quest

Now And Then

Now and then when all little Men
go to find their Self
they move in Flashes
and plunge into Gashes
seeking to learn
and to no longer yearn
for what they already are.

But better they are thus
than caught in the daily Fuss
of Concerns for Illusions
and life Diffusions
which bind them to Cycles of Sorrow and Pain
of Craving and Striving
Attaining and Hiding
and trying all over and over again.

Important To Ponder And Know

As I grow and evolve
I think
What shall I become?
or
Can I be any more
than what I already am
and always have been?

What am I that I always have been
and shall always be?

What am I really?

Concerns

Woodstock

We sat up through the Night
silent talking drinking Beer.
He had come to me
afraid to be alone
worried about his Wife
in Hospital for a difficult Birth—eventually.

We quietly talked
as we sat on the Porch
and looked onto the country Lane
that wound through the Village.

As the dark Night
yielded to Light
I sat alone on my Rocker
heavy with hours of Concern
as with my Urging
he had given in to growing Fear
and gone to be with his Wife.

continues on next page >

I saw him approach from afar
with a Weight on his Shoulder.
As he came near
I saw the white-lacquered Box
small enough to enclose
his tiny Infant.

He walked past
staring straight ahead.
We did not speak
and we never saw each other
ever again.

After the dark Night
had yielded to Light
I sat alone on my Rocker.

The Anguish Imposed By Fate

He waits in his enclosed Compound
for the shining Knight to appear
and rescue him
from the Life of Falsity he has imposed
upon himself
and others.

Alleviation of his Suffering
does not appear out of nowhere
as he aches and flails in Protest
against the Anguish imposed by Fate.
He passively crumbles
into an ever-deeper Hole.

Writhing in the Intensity of Pain
he has no Choice but to understand
the Cause of his Travails
is not Fate
but Disregard of his own Power.

continues on next page >

He is and has the Ability and Means
to respond to his inner Urgings
and conduct his Life
in Accord with who he is
and thereby fulfill himself
and profoundly contribute to Humanity.

Her Anguish

She finds herself opposing
the Truth of herself
and how she suffers and fails to function
to her Success and Fulfillment
as she shores up her Resistance
to Life in Harmony
with herself.

Her self-made Suffering
deprives her of Ease
and she feels there is Nothing she can do
to alleviate the Pain and Frustration
which grow into seizing Anger.
She seeks refuge in her Anguish.

As I Look Into Your Eyes

As I look into your Eyes
I see deep in your Core
Love and Light and the Joy of Being
you.

Glazed over that though
is a vague Veil of Disregard of yourself
the Fear of being you
the Being you truly are.

In that grey cold Emptiness
you shiver in Loneliness
as you wrap your Arms
around the empty Shell
with which you have allied yourself.

This Shell you have built
into a thick solid Wall
that encloses you
and isolates you from yourself
and from all.

continues on next page >

You cherish this Wall
and you hate it
as you distrust and fear and miss
yourself.

You yearn for the Love and Light and Joy
you know deep within
is you.

Open yourself to the Beauty and Power of Being
That You Are.

Behind My Wall

I seek Refuge
behind my Wall
which I have so carefully grown all around me
a Wall of dense Fog
and pounding Rain
and blistering Sun
while I tremble with Fear.

As I keep giving my Life
to forming this Wall
it grows thicker and higher
and robs me of Light and Life.
I gasp for the Air by which to continue
but hope it is not in the Persistence
of being separated from my true Self.

Karma

She skitters blithely
through a Life of Ignorance and Denial
leaving in her Wake
a Trail of Dysfunction and Destruction
willfully unaware of her painful Effects.

Suffering sifts through her
with insistent Force
until she finally relates it
to her Actions.
She desists and decides to change.

As she conducts her Life
more attuned to herself and others
she reaps Rewards and Healing
and returns to her dysfunctional and destructive Habits.

The Infinite Wayfarer

He steers his Vessel through myriad Galaxies
ceaselessly searching
for the Realm of Illumination and Realization.

He traverses vast interstellar Space
braves turbulent Winds and monstrous Rains
with Patience long to span the Ages.

When finally he nears his long-sought Goal
he freezes in Fear
diverts his Travels
and meanders in Hesitation
for the Remainder of his Days.

Patience-testing Times
veered astray into meaningless Tracks
toward the Nebulae of undefined Distance
removed from what lifelong Fulfillment he had sought.

continues on next page >

He loses himself in amorphous Infinity
turned away from his soul's Aspiring
and his heart's Yearning.

Soul's Dirge Of Despair

Keep me not confined in this Dungeon
with Walls of Falsity and contrived Artificiality
that hide me from the Light of Living
as they choke away
in damp dusty Darkness
the luminous Joy of being true to myself.

I wither in this Darkness
born of the Shame Fear and Anger
rotting my Core
in the Knowledge muddled by Denial
that I am the Mason who devotes this Life
to building this oppressive Wall.

continues on next page >

Sprint up full Power
born of Trust and Love of Self
and break down the Wall
now and forever
to claim who I am
with joyous Approval and Expression of Being.

Deliverance

The Road To Liberation

The Moments slide sluggish
through the heavy Night
oppressively sucking Vitality
out of enclosing Space.

He strives to rise
out of the strangulating Void
applies his Force
but Habit pulls him back.

Over the Edge of his Enclosure
he glimpses a Ray of Light
and the Color of new Life
which edges him upward.

He finds the Hope
that helps him prevail
and escape the Embrace
of his Bonds.

continues on next page >

He moves forward and onward
empowered by Choice
and by Freedom
to taste all Moments in Fullness.

He prevails no matter how long
and all within him rises
to greet the Dawn
of Ease and Home in brilliant Light.

Deliverance

The Terrors of Days
flow into Nights
Months Years
and Lives
when Fear Hunger and Pain
seem never to cease
as we endure and survive
searing Fire and burning Ice
calling upon the Permanent in us
which interconnects us all.

In Response to our Appeal
Time dawns
with Relief from Suffering,
a slow-starting Surge
of Goodness and Nurturing.

continues on next page >

Taking hold of our inner Strength
Light illumines the Days
and warms the Nights
as we embrace ourselves in unified Power
and in the Joy we have earned.

Conscious Action

Choices

What we choose to do today
will affect us now
or tomorrow
or sometime later in Life
because the Law of Cause and Effect
is unfailing.

When we function in Accord with this Law
we succeed and flourish;
in Opposition
we cause Suffering to ourselves
and others.

In The Joy Of Light

When I have a Choice
between Light and Gloom
Joy and Doom
I choose the Joy of Light
in bright Delight
for I choose not to suffer
in the Darkness
of Ignorance Isolation and Ego.

The Law Of Cause And Effect

He made his Choice
which affected his Day
or his Tomorrow
or later Life
for the Law of Cause and Effect
reliably serves Justice.

Functioning in Denial with this Directive
established by Reality
he suffers Dysfunction and Failure
no matter how hard he tries
to manipulate and pressure
the Outcome in his Favor.

continues on next page >

By acting in Harmony
with Truth Reality with what is
he assures himself of an effortless Path
toward what genuinely serves him
in a Life of real Success
effortless Balance and Peace.

Truth

Hard as Diamond
brilliant clear enduring
feared and shunned
and courted as a dazzling Beauty
oft denied seldom sought
but ever constant
Fundament of all
is Truth.

Truth shines loyally
without regard for Like or Dislike
Favor or Opposition
by the Powerful or the Weak.
It prevails in total Independence
and provides the reliable Touchstone of Reality.
Truth and Reality are One.

We Are Interconnected.

I experience myself interconnected
with all.
Thus what 'they' do
is what I do
what we do
whether we agree or not.
When I see Injustice done
I must stand up
and be counted
as one who acts for Justice.
Remaining silent and passive
we are complicit.

A Good Strategy

It is never a good Strategy
to fight Negative with Negative.
Protest not against Injustice Inequity and Falsity
with Hatred Anger and Divisiveness.
Stand up bravely and make your Actions count
with Love.
Love is the most powerful Strategy
to oppose Evil Dishonesty and even Stupidity.

Express through your Actions founded in Love
the Interconnectedness we all share.
When Breath and Life
Advancement and Opportunity
are taken from one
they are stolen from each of us.
Whether we are black or white or any other Color
is totally irrelevant.

continues on next page >

All that *is* is Being.
We All Are That.

Empathy

Hear My Heart

My Heart is heavy from Disregard.
It suffers the Agony of being treated
as if it were worthless and too little
to deserve Attention
and unconditional Love.

Hear my Heart:
I know you
and I love you.
I love the Being I am.
You are the One and the All
of what I am
and what all is.
You are the Love of Being
That I Am.

Be Still My Heart

Be still my Heart
and beat not in Fear
of being forsaken.

I will not abandon you
to Solitude and Loneliness
to long Nights of Longing
and Days of Desolation.

I am pledged to you forever
and will remain with you
in Loyalty and Acceptance
your Friend Companion and Love.

Empathy

My Heart grows weary
as in Empathy I feel the Pain and Suffering
so persistently imposed
by those who disregard their inner Knowing
of who and why they are.

They punish themselves
and disregard the innate Urgings
that attempt to remind them of the Essence
that really they are
in Power and Beauty of Being.

In this Dismissal they deprive themselves
and those they touch
in all-pervasive Interconnectedness
as one all-pervasive Being
of the lasting Pleasure and Bliss of limitless Love.

Love Glows

The Heart lies low in a dark Hollow
but Love still glows a calm burning Ember
loyally waiting
patiently preparing
for the Breath of Being
to revive the Vitality
and empower the Heart
to joyous Self-expression.

I delight in this Heart
in its Power and Fidelity
as I continue to flow through this Life
in the Joy of being Being.

I am alive
I am that I am
and that is *what* I am.
I love Being.

Evolving

Evolve Or Perish

An Organism that does not evolve
will perish.
Experience is your Guide through Evolution
by providing real Knowledge.

Learn through your learning Experiences.

Learn through your learning Experiences
and have your Knowledge empower your Actions.

And remember:
do not keep forgetting
otherwise you fail to evolve
and you will perish.

Simply Live Your Real Identity

You need not suffer
under the persistent Dictatorship of Ego.
Ego, a false Perception of your Identity,
does not really exist;
it is created as a Figment of your Imagination
and mistaken Thinking.

There is no need to fight Ego
or try to eliminate it
for it has no Existence
other than in your Creation of it.

Simply live your real Identity
by directly experiencing and expressing it
always.

The Power And Beauty Of Being

Learn about your real Identity.
This is important.
Remember and live with this Knowledge
so I do advise.
All is for Naught
without the Experience and Expression
through all your Moments and Actions
of the Power and Beauty of Being
That You Are.

Human Life

Life in the human Body
with the Ability
to see
and to hear
and touch
taste
feel
and smell

with the Ability
to perceive
and decide
and enact
in the Freedom of Self-determination
the Chosen

continues on next page >

is the most mighty Opportunity
to evolve to the highest
evolutionary Level
and experience ourselves
in limitless Interconnectedness
as all-pervasive Power of Being
in eternal Love.

Metamorphosis

When first born
into this tremulous multifarious Ocean
exposed to the Onslaught of Impulses
she responds to the essential Imperative:
survive.

She lives in the limitless primordial Soup
with all Means relating
to the Stimuli emanating
from myriad Sources
on innumerable Levels
to have her experience
that she is
and express the Reality of Being.

Not fully formed
she smiles
and creates Connection
with one who can help
with her primary Task.

continues on next page >

The Mother or Father or other Adult
responds to the Smile with Joy.
Love is born
the Link is forged
and she continues secure
with the many Steps of growing and evolving
that will ensure her Ability
to mature into Self-empowerment
and the steady Exercise of her
Ability to respond.

Secure in Response-ability
she meets all the Possibilities and Challenges
offered her by Life as a Human
and she evolves into the Realization
of self-experiencing
and self-expressing Being
dwelling in the Joy of Self-acceptance
and the lasting Peace of Consciousness.

Why Do You Tarry

Why do you tarry
while your inner Urges
summon you to respond
as Evolution calls you onward
toward Fulfillment
in the Realization
of your Potential?

You possess inherent Power
to experience and express
your true Being
in all its Glory and Beauty
free from the Shackles
of Fear Hesitation Doubt
and Distrust of Self.

continues on next page >

You have the Power
to brilliantly gloriously
be
and thrive in the Understanding and Agreement
of the Being you are.
Therein lies your lasting Liberation
your joyous Fulfillment and limitless Love.

Meditation

Endless Delight

He sits alone
with his Thoughts
as they glide and fly and slide
from one Object to another
to Memories and Anticipations
working on their own
and he forgets to be aware of himself
all that Time.

Then comes the Moment
when he remembers himself
and brings Mind back to his Center
and with it his Instruments of Perception
and Experience.
There he firmly and gently
keeps them all together
in balanced harmonious Union.

continues on next page >

His Faculties attain Quiescence.
Conflict Competition and Fluctuation cease.
There is perfect Agreement
in most refined Vibration.
Dynamic without Movement
they reflect the simple Perfection of Being
and he calmly abides in endless Delight.

Meditation

As my Path meanders
through Valleys and Peaks
I labor suffer and triumph
in Vitality and Exhaustion
as I slowly advance.

I come upon a high mountain Lake
that is tranquil and calm.
Its unruffled Waters reflect the Sun
as a perfect Orb
and my Gaze penetrates
to the very Bottom.

Thus calmed is my Mind
and assured is my Heart
in the clear Sight of my Being.
I am deeply at Peace
as I experience the Purity of Self.

Nataraja

He sits smiling subtly mellow
at Peace within himself and the World
ensconced aloft the Mountain
as Sun sets in uproarious Display of Color
and the deadly Snake of Distraction and Temptation
slithers about his Neck
to no Avail.
He is unmoved and unmoving
in total Engagement with all that is.

Focused In Serenity

She sits
amidst the Upheaval
of Moments and Movements
with her Mind torn hither and thither
followed heedlessly by her Feelings and Emotions
even her Intellect and Intuition
her Body and Senses.

She draws Mind inward
followed by the others
and has them rest in her Center
in effortless Balance
within themselves and among themselves.
Gathered and in Stillness
she steadily is.

continues on next page >

Focused in their Serenity
all her Faculties
merge with the indwelling Consciousness
that she is
like a salt Figure walking into the Ocean.
She experiences herself
as one with all.

Dwelling In The Unalloyed Experience Of Self

I dwell in the unalloyed Experience of Self
not seeking Refuge in
Complication Distortion Knowing and Not-knowing
accepting the Being I Am
free of Conditions Distractions and Exceptions
fulfilled in the Purity and Joy of the Power of Being.

Secure and at Peace in this State
my Mind Feelings and Emotions
are bathed in the Fullness of Tranquility.
I abide in lasting Peace.

The Eternal Now

Being
in the Poise of effortless Balance
I experience Self
aware that I am
Being.

I am Being
aware of being
Being aware of being aware
that I am
aware of Self.

I delight in the Knowledge
that I am
the Power of Being
in infinite Experience
true to Self.

continues on next page >

I blissfully savor the Experience of Self
the Essence
that I am
the Power to be
that is the Essence of all.

I calmly dwell
in the Joy of Infinitude
the transcendent Power of Being
all-pervasive and eternal
That I Am.

Abiding Love

I feel warmed
with Light and Love
from my Core to the Surface
in the Clarity of Oneness
that I experience
in the Consciousness of Being
that is my Essence
and the Source of all that is.

I dwell in the calm Joy of Being
in unconditional Agreement
with the real Identity
that I am.
This is the direct Wellspring
whence flows
the continuous calm Pleasure
of abiding in Self.

Interconnected Being

In The Garden

A Garden refines our Sensibilities
and stimulates our finer Abilities
to subtly sense and separate
the Superficial from the Substantial
the Artificial from the Natural
the merely Functional from the Sublime.

In our Garden we dwell in Harmony
among our mind's Perceptions
our feelings' Experiences
and our body's Actions.

A Garden is grown
of Earth Water and Love
expressing the blossoming Beauty
of the timeless Soul.

A beautiful Garden soothes the savaged Soul
as Nature bestows her gentle Nurturing.

In the Wild
Nature can be an unforgiving destructive Mistress;
in the Garden
Nature gives of herself as a generous nurturing Mother.

The Garden silently invites us
into her healing Embrace
where our Spirit comes to the Fore
free empowered whole.

In the Garden we are gifted
with nature's Generosity
which inspires us to savor life's Blessings
from the Simple to the Sublime.

≈≈≈

A Garden is a fit Home
for the unfettered Soul.

The Garden
frees the Mind
delights the Senses
refreshes the Body
and heals the whole Being.

In a Garden
we join our Energies
with nature's creative Forces
to compose a Symphony
that sings of the pure Power
of Earth Sky and Water
and the human Soul.

ଛଡ଼ଡ଼ଡ଼

The imagined Limitations of being human
are gently and persistently transcended
as we join our Forces with Nature
in creating or savoring a Garden.

A Garden
liberates us from the Ordinary
expands our Experience
broadens our Horizons
and helps us to become better
at being who we are.

The Splashing of the Waters
is the Voice of Nature
singing her Delight in Being.

৯৵৯৵৯৵

The Garden provides a harmonious Union
between our physical Senses
and our spiritual Sensibility.

As a Friend mirrors our Personality
so a Garden reflects our Soul.

ೋೋೋ

May all who into this Garden go
be uplifted by nature's Gifts
that herein grow.
May your Body and Mind
and your Spirit be set right
as you walk and reflect
in this Garden of Delight.

Busy Bee

The Bee hums through the World
busily buzzing
from Bloom to Bloom
she gathers and she gives
life Elixir
ever ardent active constant.

She is one with her Hive
and contributes without Hesitation
her delightful Offering
of sweet Nectar
and life-spreading Influence
asking nothing in Return.

Living The Light

All This I Am

Water falling Birds rising Wind blowing
all this Beauty
all this Grandeur
all this Wind and Sky
all the blue massive Mountains
delicate Flowers
all this I am.

All this I am
even this Body and its Sensations
Feelings and Thoughts
all this I am
and you sitting next to me
all you about me
all of you I am.

continues on next page >

I am the Sound of Water falling
and the Birds of the Air
the Hardness of the granite Mountains
and the Delicacy of the beautiful mountain Flowers
even the brilliant Whiteness of the Snow
contrasted with the dark Shadows of the Mountains
am I
wrapped with powder Blueness of Sky
That I Am.

Mirror Light

I bathe in the beautiful Light
that glows deep within my Core
and shines forth in all Directions
as it illuminates all.
This Light is reflected from all it touches
and returns to me
as the Light
That I Am.

Absorbed In The Light Of Being

Choose to be absorbed in the Experience
of the Light of Being that you are
reflected by all that surrounds you—
the Earth and Sky
the Waters and Mountains
every Creature and Plant
each Blade of Grass
each Cell.

Love

A Perfect Romantic Moment

The full Moon shone silver
reflected as a perfect Orb upon the tranquil Lake
during the Night of the new Year.
It was quiet,
the surrounding Rajasthani Villages asleep.
We walked transfixed
floating through the magical Scene
as we meandered around the luminous Lake.
A Donkey peacefully walked near us
and stopped to calmly take us in.

The Dance of Creation

The Galaxies and every Atom
in their Dance of Creation
reflect the Power and Beauty of Being
That You Are.

Liberation

I allow Everything about me
to reflect Awareness of myself
as eternal Consciousness.
I give to each Part of me a deep Sense
of limitless Self
and thereby liberate myself
from Fear Anxiety Anger and Blame.
As I am sincerely and fully present
I gaze unto the magnificent loving Self I am:
I am conscious Being.

You Are My All

As the Dawn touches the Lids of my Eyes
I feel you
you are my All.

As I am aroused to Wakefulness
I think of you
I love you
you are my All.

As I go through each Day and each Night
I live in you
you are my All.

You are the All of me
the All of all that is
my Substance my Essence my Being
you are my All.

Concert

Our multifarious Vibrations
flow in richly layered Unity
exploring
expressing
the limitless Wealth
of our Oneness
as we dance and sing
and know our Being.

Being soars
in unfettered Bliss
reveling in the harmonious Unity
that
in Multiformity and Indivisibility
I
self-knowingly
am.

We Have Each Other

When Danger rages
and threatens Deprivation and Limitation
when we face Fear and Sorrow
remember we have each other
and we shall prevail.

When Winds whirl wild
or Sun sizzles without Mercy
and we sweat and shiver
remember we have each other
and we shall flourish in Interconnectedness.

When Disease saps us
when Weakness and Pain prevail
when we are exhausted and hurting
remember we have each other
and we shall rise with Commitment and Courage.

continues on next page >

When we feel isolated and lonely
unknown and unappreciated
and we writhe in Despair
remember we have each other
and we shall advance
our Hearts filled with Love.

I Give Thanks

I give Thanks for this Food and Drink
and for this Moment of Being
and for all Moments of Being.

I give Thanks for the Power and Beauty
of all that I have
and all that I am.

I give Thanks.

Sweet Death

A Wave

A Wave
I am a Wave a Wave.

She expressed me
from deep within her Loins
my Mother the Ocean
and flung me forth
upon her endless frothy Breast
a Wave
I am a Wave a Wave.

I have grown into my Form
and play and fight
with the others
as I become more distinct
myself
a Wave
I am a Wave a Wave.

continues on next page >

As I rear myself proudly above the Ocean
I forget my Source
and I move ever further
through glittering hot Day
and through star-spangled Night
as I cry out my Loneliness
a Wave
I am a Wave a Wave.

On one dark turbulent Night
I rear up in Fright
when I see myself hurtling heedlessly
toward the sharp-rocked Shore.
I know my Fate
as I see others before me
dashed to Oblivion
against unyielding Stone
a Wave
I am a Wave a Wave.

continues on next page >

I helplessly dash onward
to my Annihilation
in the Frenzy of Fear
which at last I bring to Stillness.
I meet jagged and round Rock
and give up my Form
of the Wave
the Wave that Wave.

I immerse myself again
in the cooling Depth
of mother Ocean
and realize that
I am that
I am the infinite Ocean
I am that I am
I am.

What Death Has Me Ask

When I come to the End of this Life
what can I say
that I have worked out
and
if I had additional Time
what would I still have to do
to be able to declare
I have fulfilled the Reason
for coming into this Life?

Oh Death

Oh Death
beloved Purifier
you cleared the Field with your Fire
to make room for my Birth
into Illumination.
For this I thank you.

Oh sweet Teacher
you came to me
a Child of six
and helped me gather my Forces
and my Attention
unto my Life.
For this I thank you.

You taught me
oh Death
to restrain myself from Behaviors and Actions
contrary to myself
and focus upon my Growth toward Fulfillment.
For this I thank you.

continues on next page >

Throughout my Life
you have not let me forget you.
You have been my constant Companion
my Guide
who quietly and calmly
nudges me toward ever-greater Heights and Depths
of being in Touch with the Fullness
the Essence
the Source of me
of you
and of all.
For this I thank you.

Oh my sweet Love
throughout my Life
you have given me Meaning.
You have called me to see beyond my imagined Limits
and gain the Fullness of Life
oh Death.
For this I thank you.

In your Constancy
you have been my most reliable and loyal Companion.
For this I thank you.

continues on next page >

You have held before me oh Death
the greatest of all Boons
that has given my Life Direction and Beauty:
the Boon of merging in divine Consciousness
to live eternally in the Light
of unending Joy
and the Experience of limitless Union.
For this I thank you.

You oh Death my Love
are the living Promise of my Delivery
to infinite Freedom
and abiding Bliss.
For this I thank you.

Going Home

When the Infinite knows
in his limitless Wisdom
that we his Children
have fulfilled our Purpose for being on Earth
he fulfills his Promise
and returns us to our original Home
at his Side.

Free To Fly Past Stars And Galaxies

I rest on the Grass
Hands laced behind Head
Eyes open to Sky
blue clear Light
and I wonder
how much longer will I be
in this Life on Earth
and how will Death take me:
in my Sleep peacefully
or in a Moment while working or playing
or laughing with someone in joyous Embrace?
Will I experience Death?
That would be good.

I welcome you Death
my life-long Companion and Teacher
and I will lovingly walk with you
as you conduct me into the next Realm
aware that I continue to be.
I love to be and move with you
into the Beyond.

continues on next page >

I loved it as I walked through the Valleys of this Realm
and the Mountains and Oceans and Skies
and I welcome you Death
as you guide me into limitless Space and eternal Time
free to fly past Stars and Galaxies
into the Joy of endless Being.

Now I Lie Here Sweet Death

Now I lie here sweet Death
in your Arms
and ask you to deliver me
to the Realm of Peace and Light and Love.
You have been by my Side constantly
throughout my Life
and have gently secretly guided me
to this Time of Opportunity
when you bring me Home
to be one with all I love
in eternal Peace and Joy.

I Am

I Am Infinite Being

Om
I Am Being
Infinite Being
All-Pervasive And Eternal
I Am
Om

I Am

In all Phenomena
and every Being
I know Self
the Power of Being that I am
that we all are.

Through the Brilliance of the Sun
as well as the gentle Glow of a Candle
I know that I am.

Through the Crescendo of Thunder
as well as the quietest Hum
I know that I am.

Through the Hardness of Rock
and through the Softness of Sand
I know that I am.

Through the Fluidity of Water
and through the Intangibility of Space
through the Infinitude of Consciousness
I know that I am.

continues on next page >

Through the interstellar Winds
as well as the Breath I draw
I know that I am.

I take Note of this Breath
for it is the Expression
of the universal Power of Being I am
the Flow of that Force which never shall cease.

I trace the in-taken Breath
to the Cave of my Heart
to the Center of Being that I am.

Where is the Center of Infinity?
Anywhere.
Where is the Center of the infinite Cosmos?
Everywhere.

continues on next page >

I experience the Cave of my Heart
 as the Center of the Cosmos
  and know my Self
   in Infinity
   in Eternity
   in Reality.

I Am That

The Power of Being *is*
everywhere all the Time and all that is.
All that *is* is Being.
I dwell in the Experience of Being
that I am
I am that
Being is.

I am Being.
Being is pure Energy
Essence of all.
Energy is indestructible and indivisible
eternally and all-pervasively continuous.
I am Being.

Being and the Ability to know Self are inseparable—
what good would it be for all that is
to be
without the Ability to experience Self?
Being and Self-experience are inseparable
they are one.

continues on next page >

The Experience of Self is Consciousness.
Being and Consciousness
are one.
Being is Consciousness.
I am Being
I am Consciousness.

Self-knowing Being
is in absolute Agreement with Self:
this is the Seed of Love.
Self-acceptance is Love
that is Bliss.
I dwell in the Experience of Being
infinite Consciousness absolute Bliss
that I am.
BeingConsciousnessBlissAbsolute
is my true Identity
That I Am
I Am That.

Experiencing Being Together

I conclude here
in the Hope that we experienced together
and dwelled lovingly in Union
and in the Light and Joy of Being.

Photograph Captions
PHOTOGRAPHS BY ERHARD VOGEL*

Cover
Sketch
By Erhard

Page 1
Erhard
(*Photographer anonymous)

Page 7
Afghanistan

Page 25
Nataraja's Arm
Sculpture by Erhard
Nataraja Ashram

Page 31
Pagoda
Germany

Page 45
Village Women At Lake
Udaipur, India

Page 55
Cliff Carving
Afghanistan

Page 69
Kabul
Afghanistan

Page 85
Nataraja Ashram Garden

Page 105
Winter Birches
New York State

Page 113
Karin & Erhard
Donauwörth, Germany
(*Photographer anonymous)

Page 129
Stream Scene
South Carolina

Page 147
Soest
Germany

About The Author

Erhard Vogel, PhD, is recognized as one of the foremost meditation and Self-realization teachers in the world. Born in war-torn Germany, Dr. Vogel immigrated to the United States at age fourteen. He graduated from the Pratt Institute of Design in New York and at an early age rose to a respected position in a world-renowned architectural firm. At thirty-one he set aside a brilliant career in architecture to devote himself to the service of humanity.

For four years Erhard, as he likes to be called by his students, traveled the globe on foot. He lived in Europe, the Middle East, Afghanistan, India, Nepal and China, thoroughly researching the ways in which people of different cultures seek fulfillment. He saw the underlying need in everyone to fulfill their potential.

In India Erhard met two of the world's most renowned luminous Masters, who welcomed him into their midst and invited him to teach among the Himalayan sages—a rare distinction for a Westerner. He lived for an extended period in a Himalayan cave in a remote sacred area.

Living in utter joy and luminosity, Erhard remembered how so many throughout the world suffer. He returned home to address the problems and aspirations of our contemporary society with his teachings. Following a lecture tour spanning the United States, Europe and Canada, he came to San Diego and founded the Nataraja Yoga Ashram, a not-for-profit social service organization.

Erhard's teachings are a unique combination of time-tested wisdom and pragmatic method. His fundamental, experiential, systematic approach is based upon sound psychological, physiological and spiritual principles that make meditation and Self-realization practical and attainable.

Erhard teaches not from books nor from other people's ideas but out of his own profound life experience. Through his depth of knowledge he is able to inspire and gently guide sincere students to the experience of their limitless potential. With unconditional acceptance and unwavering respect for the Being they are, he inspires his students to recognize their real Self and to treat themselves with trust and kindness.

Since 1969 Erhard has taught tens of thousands of students throughout the world. He continues to travel regularly to India and teach among the sages in the Himalayas, where he is recognized as a Master Teacher. He has authored four additional books: *Self-Healing Through The Awareness Of Being*; *Journey Into Your Center*; *The Four Gates: A Saga Of The Human Being On The Path From The Pit Of Despair To The Realm Of Fulfillment, From Confusion To Clarity, Culminating In The Deepest Realization*; and *A Dialogue With Death The Teacher Of Life: An Ancient Story For The Modern World*; as well as numerous audio recordings of guided meditations and teachings. Erhard currently offers courses through the Ashram in San Diego, California.

Also By Erhard Vogel

Books:

*A Dialogue With Death The Teacher Of Life:
An Ancient Story For The Modern World*

The Four Gates: A Saga Of The Human Being On The Path From The Pit Of Despair To The Realm Of Fulfillment, From Confusion To Clarity, Culminating In The Deepest Realization

Journey Into Your Center

Self-Healing Through The Awareness Of Being
(out of print)

Audio Recordings of Guided Meditations and Teachings:

The Cave Meditation

*The Stress Release Response:
Seven Steps To Triumph Over Stress*

Guided Meditation For Beginners

Centering Meditation

Feelings And Emotions

The Healing Power Of Love

The Silent Observer

*Yoga For Life:
Two Hours Of Guided Yoga Classes
(Basic And Advanced)*

*Advanced Breathing Technique
and The Breath Meditation*

www.ingramcontent.com/pod-product-compliance
Lightning Source LLC
Chambersburg PA
CBHW050027130526
44590CB00042B/2028